ALL ABOUT...

THE
Great Fire

OF LONDON

PAM ROBSON

Text © Pam Robson 1996

Illustrations © Dez Marwood 1996

Photographs © Sources credited

© Macdonald Young Books Ltd 1996

First published in Great Britain in 1996 by Macdonald Young Books

61 Western Road, Hove, East Sussex, BN3 1JD

A CIP catalogue for this book is available from the British Library.

ISBN 0 7500 1824 0 (hbk) 0 7500 1935 2 (pbk)

Editor: Annie Scothern

Designer: Jane Hannath

Picture credits: Mary Evans Picture Library - *cover, title page, 8, 10, 21, 24, 27r, 29, 33, 37t, 39t, 45.*
Museum of London - *9, 11, 13, 16, 22, 27l, 30, 32, 34, 36, 37b, 42, 43, 44.* The Bridgeman Art Library - *25.*
The Guildhall Library - *18, 19, 31, 35.* The Mansell Collection - *20.* James Stevenson - *12, 15, 17, 38, 40,
41.* The Times Newspapers Limited 1994, 'Thatching underway on the Globe theatre' - *39b.*

The author and publishers thank the above for permission to reproduce their photographs.

Printed and bound in Belgium by Proost N.V.

Other titles in the *ALL ABOUT...* series:

THE COMING OF THE RAILWAYS

THE GREAT PLAGUE

THE FIRST WORLD WAR

MACDONALD YOUNG BOOKS

TIMELINE

AD 64 *Rome burns*

1087 *The Saxon church of St Paul is destroyed by fire*
1189 *A law is passed in England stating houses should be built of stone*
1212 *A fire in London kills 3,000 people*

1555 *Nostradamus's first almanac*
1633 *Buildings north of London Bridge are destroyed by fire*
1660 *Samuel Pepys begins to write his diary*
1665 *The Great Plague*
1666
    2 September *The Great Fire of London breaks out*
    3 September *Pepys and his wife flee from their home in their night clothes*
    4 September *St Paul's Cathedral burns down*
    5 September *The fire is under control; John Evelyn sees homeless people all around London*
    7 September *Evelyn finds the ground still hot under his feet*
    16 September *Plans for the rebuilding of the City are submitted by Sir Christopher Wren and John Evelyn*
    1667 *Rebuilding Act; fire insurance begins*
    1677 *The Monument to the Great Fire is completed*

1710 *The first service is held in the new St Paul's Cathedral*
1861 *A large fire south of London Bridge burns for four days*
1871 *Chicago burns*
1940 *St Paul's Cathedral survives German bombs during the Second World War; a national fire service emerges during the war years*

CONTENTS

CITIES ABLAZE

In AD 64 the city of Rome burned for six days. Tacitus, an eyewitness, reported that: "It began in the Circus [stadium]...breaking out in shops selling inflammable goods, and fanned by the wind, the conflagration instantly grew...The ancient city's narrow winding streets...encouraged its progress." The Roman Emperor Nero later blamed Christians for starting the fire. The multi-storeyed houses of Rome contained massive wooden beams and frequently caught fire.

These are some of the cities of the world that have had to be rebuilt because they were destroyed by fire.

Groups of firefighting night-watchmen called *vigiles* patrolled the streets. After this fire some of the buildings in Rome were rebuilt in stone. There were many similarities between Rome before the fire of AD 64 and London in 1666.

Pliny the Elder used the word 'sipho' in Ancient Roman times to describe a fire engine. He probably meant a siphon-squirt like this one. These were used during the Roman occupation of Britain and were still in use when the Great Fire of London broke out.

FIGHTING FIRES

Householders in Ancient Rome were expected to have firefighting tools such as water buckets, hooks, ladders and axes in case of fire. Long-handled hooks were particularly useful – these were needed to pull down burning roofs.

This type of wheeled firefighting equipment may have been used to fight the Great Fire of London.

This is a model of a fire engine being carried to the scene of the fire!

After the collapse of the Roman Empire, little progress was made in the development of effective firefighting equipment until the 16th century when a giant water-squirting siphon was developed in Germany. The water came from a barrel that had to be filled by emptying buckets of water into it. By 1666 some further improvements had been made but not enough to deal with the inferno that was the Great Fire.

A wooden ladder found in Roman Britain.

LIVING WITH FIRE

F ire was a constant threat in ancient cities like Rome. In the Middle Ages, Londoners also recognised it as a familiar hazard that they had to live with. Only a few details can be found of the fires that London suffered before 1666. In the 10th century the whole City of London was destroyed. Between the years of 1077 and 1135, seven major fires broke out. In the fire of 1212, 3,000 people were said to have died.

London in the mid-1660s was much smaller than it is today. Most of the poor people lived in the 'square mile' (known as the 'City of London') inside the old City walls. When the Great Fire broke out, people were able to flee to surrounding fields.

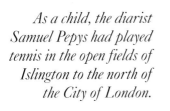

In 1633 a massive fire destroyed a block of buildings to the north of London Bridge. When rebuilding took place, a firebreak was left. This later prevented the flames of the Great Fire of 1666 from reaching south of the River Thames. The chronicler William Fitz Stephen wrote in 1180: "The only plagues of London...are the immoderate drinking of fools and the frequency of fires."

Attempts were made to introduce fire precautions in London. Each parish in the City had to provide buckets, hand-squirts, and hooks to pull down smouldering thatch.

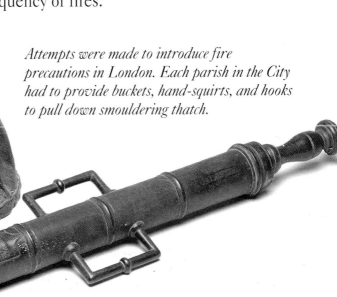

FIRE WIPES OUT PLAGUE

U sing eyewitness accounts and contemporary paintings and engravings, historians have put together a picture of London on the evening of Saturday 1 September 1666. Lumbering wagons squeezed their way through the narrow streets, with fights often breaking out between drivers over right of way. There were no pavements. Wooden bollards lined the streets. Filth and sewage, stinking in the hot dry weather, lay waiting to be cleared by 'rakers'.

St Olave's is one of the few City churches that survived the Great Fire. Samuel Pepys, an eyewitness to the fire, lived close by in Seething Lane. The skulls on the church gate are a reminder of victims of a plague in 1658 who are buried there.

A rare view of London before it was destroyed by the Great Fire of 1666.

The Great Plague was still causing deaths, although the worst was over. An easterly wind arose. At some time after midnight the Great Fire began. It was to clear the last remnants of plague left in London.

Pepys kept a famous diary in which he recorded details about the Great Plague of 1665 and the Great Fire of London in 1666. This monument to him can still be seen inside St Olave's church.

A FRESH EAST WIND

The City of London was asleep when the easterly wind blew up in the early hours of Sunday 2 September. There had been a long hot spell without rain and everything was as dry as tinder. The wind fanned a few sparks from the premises of Thomas Farynor, master baker of Pudding Lane.

Samuel Pepys recorded in his diary: "...Jane called us up about three in the morning, to tell us of a great fire they saw in the city... I thought it far enough off; and so went to bed again, and to sleep." Fortunately for Pepys, his home in Seething Lane escaped the flames.

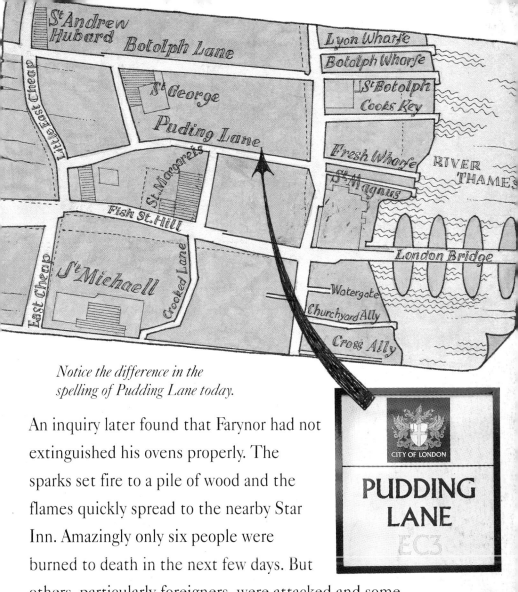

Notice the difference in the spelling of Pudding Lane today.

An inquiry later found that Farynor had not extinguished his ovens properly. The sparks set fire to a pile of wood and the flames quickly spread to the nearby Star Inn. Amazingly only six people were burned to death in the next few days. But others, particularly foreigners, were attacked and some were murdered. England was at war with Holland at the time and there were people who believed that the Dutch were responsible for starting the fire.

FUEL FOR THE FIRE

Tinder-dry wooden buildings in narrow dirty streets, together with the strong east wind, created ideal conditions for a fire to spread rapidly. Many houses in 17th-century London were multi-storeyed – like those in Ancient Rome. Open coal or wood fires provided heat and light, and candles burned in many windows at night. Fire regulations had been introduced but they were often ignored. As far back as 1189, a law had stated that houses were to be built of stone and roofs were to be covered with slates or tiles. King James I had encouraged building with bricks, while Charles II ordered the imprisonment of anyone who put up a timber-framed building.

This picture of the old London Bridge shows a 17th-century timber-framed building.

A cross-section through a typical timber-framed house of 17th-century London.

But it made no difference. Bricks and stone were expensive so London remained a wooden city. Even thatched roofs could still be seen.

Medieval buildings like the Staple Inn can still be seen in London.

17

PIPED WATER

At the time of the Great Fire, the southern part of the City of London had a piped water supply. Water was pumped from the River Thames through pipes, some made out of hollowed tree trunks, to taps in the streets. This water supply might have been useful in helping to put out the flames. But there had been a drought over the summer months and water levels were unusually low.

Waterwheels under the last arch of London Bridge drove a pump that raised water from the river. This water was pumped through a lead pipe by St Magnus's church, then along wooden conduit pipes up Fish Street Hill and Grace Church (Gracious) Street.

To the west of the City of London, the people of Westminster also had a public water supply – the overflow from the fountain in the centre of New Palace Yard!

In addition, within the first few hours of the outbreak of fire the waterworks that pumped the water direct from the Thames were set alight. The machinery collapsed into the river and London burned out of control.

In the 17th century, street-sellers sold 'fresh river water'.

GUARDING THE STREETS

The streets of 17th-century London held many dangers. Most people preferred to travel along the river. At night elderly watchmen patrolled the dark, unlit streets but there was no police force. Orders issued by the king or the Lord Mayor of London were carried out by officials known as 'constables'. The people were expected to help extinguish any fires that broke out. Church bells rang a warning and everyone hurried to collect firefighting equipment.

In the 17th century, watchmen helped with firefighting.

The militia were bands of Londoners who were trained to use weapons in times of war.

When the Great Fire started, most of the people were more concerned to escape with their belongings than to stop the flames. This was one reason why the fire caught hold and raged for several days. No organised firefighting began until the king took command and ordered soldiers and the militia to help.

People fled to the river as the fire took hold.

FORETELLING THE FIRE

ostradamus had produced his first almanac containing his predictions in 1555. A century later, science and magic were still closely linked together. Astrologers foretold the future. Samuel Pepys consulted William Lilly, a famous astrologer and almanac-maker of the time. Lilly predicted the Great Fire of London.

William Lilly

An inscription on the monument that commemorates the Great Fire blamed Papists (Catholics) for starting it. This was the result of pressure on the Government when anti-Catholic feeling was strong. The inscription was finally removed in 1830.

HERE BY Y PERMISSION OF HEAVEN, HELL BROKE LOOSE UPON THIS PROTESTANT CITY FROM THE MALICIOUS HEARTS OF BARBAROUS PAPISTS, BY Y HAND OF THEIR AGENT HUBERT, WHO CONFESSED, AND ON Y RUINES OF THIS PLACE DECLARED THE FACT, FOR WHICH HE WAS HANGED, (VIZT) THAT HERE BEGAN THAT DRED-FULL FIRE, WHICH IS DESCRIBED AND PERPETUATED ON AND BY THE NEIGHBOURING PILLAR. Erected Anno 168_ in the Majoraltie of S^R P_TIENCE WARD K^t

Robert Hubert, a French Roman Catholic, claimed to have started the Great Fire. Anti-Catholic feelings were running high and Hubert was hanged, even though his confession was untrue.

When his prediction came true, Lilly found himself accused of starting the fire! On 13 December 1666 Pepys wrote: "...and the fire did indeed break out on the 2nd of September; which is very strange methinks." An inquiry held on 25 September 1666 into the causes of the Great Fire reported that: "...nothing has been found to argue the fire in London to have been caused by other than the hand of God, a great wind and a very dry season."

THE FLAMES TAKE HOLD

During the first day of the Great Fire, little action was taken to prevent the fire from spreading. When Samuel Pepys had first woken at 3 a.m., the fire had reached Fish Street Hill. From there it was blown south and west towards the River Thames. The Lord Mayor of London, Thomas Bludworth, had reacted in a similar way to Pepys – he had returned to bed, commenting: "Pish, a woman could piss it out." Meanwhile the easterly wind swept the flames onwards, badly damaging St Margaret's church and destroying the church of St Magnus and the Thames waterworks.

Along the Thames riverside were tall warehouses full of oil, sugar, butter, tar, brandy and other inflammable goods. The flames reached them – and what had been a local fire developed into the inferno that raged through London for the next three days.

People fled with their belongings to the open spaces surrounding the City of London. Pepys saw: "...people fleeing [the fire] and nobody endeavouring to quench it, but to remove their goods and leave all to the fire."

Fortunately the flames did not sweep across London Bridge. But it was not until lunchtime that the Lord Mayor finally agreed to the demolition of houses to create firebreaks.

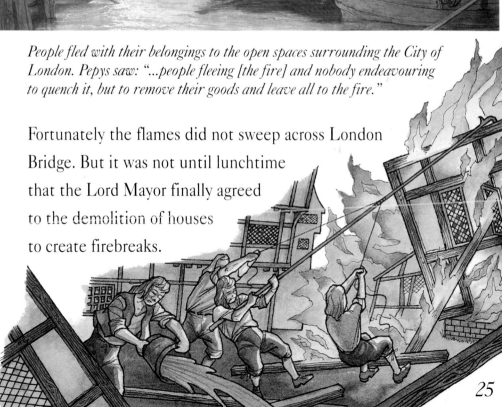

EYEWITNESSES

U nlike the previous Lord Mayor of London, who had shown great courage during the worst months of the Great Plague, Thomas Bludworth was not a man of action. There was an old law which stated that whoever ordered the demolition of houses to create firebreaks had to pay all the rebuilding costs. So the Lord Mayor put off taking the decision. When Samuel Pepys finally rose from his bed on the Sunday morning, his maid reported that 300 houses had already burned down. Pepys left his home and walked to the Tower of London.

Historians have created a detailed picture of the major events of the Great Fire from eyewitness accounts. The most famous accounts are the diaries of Samuel Pepys, Clerk to the Navy, and the diaries of his great friend John Evelyn.

From there he could see houses at the end of London Bridge on fire. He then travelled by boat to London Bridge and saw Londoners fleeing the city.

JOHN EVELYN

"...all the sky were of a fiery aspect, like the top of a burning oven and the light seen about forty miles around for many nights. London was, but is no more."

(Describing the burning of St Paul's Cathedral:)

"...the melting lead running down the streets in a stream, and the very pavements glowing with a fiery redness, so as now horse nor man was able to tread on them..."

SAMUEL PEPYS

"...poor people staying in their houses as long as till the very fire touched them, and then, running into boats, or clambering from one pair of stairs, by the waterside, to another. And among other things, the poor pigeons, I perceived, were loath to leave their houses, but hovering about the windows and balconies till they burned their wings and fell down."

"...everything after so long a drought, proving combustible, even the very stones of the churches."

"...but Lord, what a sad sight it was by moonlight to see the whole City on fire almost..."

THE KING TAKES CHARGE

C oncerned at the Lord Mayor's lack of action and the speed at which the flames were travelling, Pepys went to see the king later on the Sunday. King Charles immediately issued orders for the demolition of all houses in the path of the fire. On Monday 3 September at 4 a.m., Pepys and his wife gathered together some of their belongings and left their home in Seething Lane, riding on a cart in their night-clothes. On the same day the king overturned any laws that might be stopping effective action against the fire.

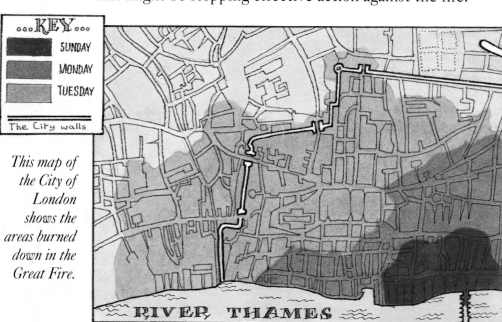

KEY

SUNDAY

MONDAY

TUESDAY

The City walls

This map of the City of London shows the areas burned down in the Great Fire.

RIVER THAMES

In 1979, archaeologists discovered 20 charred barrels from the 17th century lying on racks in a cellar close to Pudding Lane. A burnt substance covering them was found to be pitch, which is highly inflammable.

Fireposts were set up, manned by soldiers and civilians. The firefighters were directed by the king's brother – James, Duke of York.

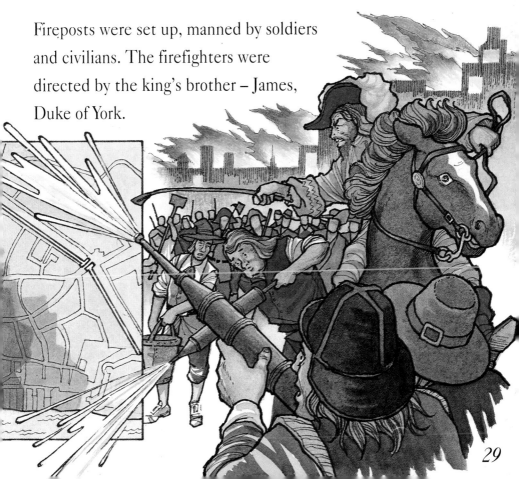

TUESDAY 4 SEPTEMBER

O n the third day of the Great Fire, King Charles was riding through the burning streets. Suddenly he leapt from his horse to help with the firefighting effort. Dirty and mud-stained, he passed buckets of water and wielded an axe to create firebreaks. He rewarded the brave actions of other people with gold coins from his purse.

"IN SIXTEEN HUNDRED AND SIXTY SIX, LONDON BURNED LIKE ROTTEN STICKS."

Although the king's actions restored order at a time of public fear and panic, they failed to stop the progress of the fire. Samuel Pepys removed more belongings from his home – even burying some important papers, wine and Parmesan cheese in the garden of his friend Sir William Penn.

During the Great Plague of 1665, the king had fled from London. But now he was seen as the hero of the hour.

FLAMES ENGULF ST PAUL'S

During the night of Tuesday 4 September, the wind dropped and changed direction to become a gentle northerly breeze. By the evening of Wednesday 5 September the fire was under control, although it still smouldered in isolated patches all the next day. It was finally halted to the west of the City. A charred wilderness remained, with fewer than one-sixth of London's buildings still standing. Most of the 97 parish churches had been destroyed, including St Paul's Cathedral. About 13,200 houses, 400 streets and 44 of the 51 City of London company halls had been consumed by the flames, as well as inns, prisons and warehouses.

This 17th-century house sign of 'Gerard the Giant' is made of painted wood. Gerard's Hall in Basing Lane was destroyed by the fire. After 1666, house signs made from stone started to appear.

The fire ended here.

This Boy is in Memmory Putt up for the late FIRE of LONDON Occasion'd by the Sin of Gluttony 1666

St Paul's Cathedral in flames.

This statue was put up in Cock Lane to mark the spot where the fire ended.

THE AFTERMATH

O n Wednesday 5 September John Evelyn saw many homeless people in St George's fields, to the south of London Bridge, and in Moorfields, to the north of the City. Once again the king took command and issued emergency proclamations. Soldiers were ordered to clear fire debris. People who had lost their homes in the fire were provided with food and tents.

The people of Cowfold in the south of England sent 53 shillings and ninepence to the Lord Mayor's disaster fund.

Received the 26th day of November 1666, of Mr Thomas Lintott returned from Cowfold in Sussex the Summe of fifty three shillings & Nine pence which was collected in the said Parish on the Fast Day, being the 10th day of October 1666. towards the Relief of those Persons who have been great Sufferers by the late Sad Fire within the City of London.

Sa: Kendall

On Friday 7 September John Evelyn observed:
"I went this morning on foot from Whitehall as far as London Bridge...with extraordinary difficulty, clambering over heaps of yet smoking rubbish...the ground under my feet so hot, that it even burnt the soles of my shoes..."

Royal proclamation,
5 September 1666.

Towns and villages
around the City of
London were ordered to
take in refugees. The
Lord Mayor launched a
disaster fund and money
flowed in from all over
Britain.

By the King,
A PROCLAMATION
For the keeping of Markets to supply the City of *London* with Provisions,
and also for prevention of Alarms and Tumults, and for appointing the
Meeting of Merchants.

CHARLES R.

Whereas most of the places wherein Markets were kept in our City of London are destroyed by the late fire, We are desirous, That Our loving Subjects may nevertheless be furnished with a constant Supply of Provisions, as well as the present Exigency will permit: It is therefore Our will and pleasure, That Markets be kept and held within and without Bishops-gate, at Towerhill, and Smithfield every day of the week, and also continued in Leaden-hall-street upon the days wherein they have been accustomed to be held. Requiring all persons whom it may concern, duely and constantly to resort unto the places, and at the times above mentioned, We having taken care to secure the said Markets in safety, and prevent all disturbance by refusal of payment for their Goods, or otherwise. And We do further charge and command all Mayors, Sheriffs, Justices of the Peace, and other Our Officers and Ministers within the Counties from whence Provisions are or have been usually brought to Our said City of London, to take notice of this Our will and pleasure, and to use their utmost diligence and authority to see the same performed accordingly.

And whereas through the temerity and unadvisedness of some persons, groundless fears and apprehensions have been and may be cast into the minds of our people, to prevent all Tumults and Disorders which may thereby or otherwise arise, it is Our will and pleasure, That upon any Alarm raised or taken, no man stir or disquiet himself by reason thereof, but only attend the business of quenching the fire. We having in our Princely Care taken order to draw together such a sufficient force both of Horse and Foot in and about Our said City, as may abundantly secure the peace and safety thereof, and prevent attempts any Attempts whatsoever that can be made to disturbe the same.

And whereas the Royal Exchange is demolished and burned down by the late fire, It is Our pleasure, that Gresham College in Bishops-gate street be for the present the place for the usual meeting and assembling of Merchants in the same manner as heretofore the Exchange was. Given at Our Court at Whitehall the fifth day of September 1666. in the Eighteenth year of Our Reign.

God save the KING.

I then went towards Islington and Highgate, where one might
have seen 200,000 people of all ranks and degrees dispersed and
lying along by their heaps of what they could save from the fire,
deploring their loss and ready to perish from hunger and
destitution..."

ST PAUL'S CATHEDRAL

S t Paul's Cathedral was already in a state of disrepair before the Great Fire. When the flames took hold, it was completely destroyed. The only monument that survived and can still be seen

In 1087 the Saxon church of St Paul was destroyed by fire. The new cathedral, completed in 1327, was the longest in northern Europe. At 140 metres high, the spire dominated London's skyline.

today is the statue of the poet John Donne. Scorch marks are still visible on it. The present St Paul's was designed by Sir Christopher Wren and built between 1675 and 1710. The main material used in its construction was Portland stone from the south of England. Wren was already a famous mathematician and astronomer before he became an architect.

St Paul's Cathedral, designed by Christopher Wren.

At the time that London had to be rebuilt, Wren was the leading building designer. On 16 September 1666, Wren and Evelyn each presented plans for a new City of London to the king.

Nearly 300 years after the Great Fire, St Paul's Cathedral burned again – ignited by firebombs during the Second World War. This time it was saved.

BUILDING REGULATIONS

There were homeless people to rehouse and churches, inns, shops, administrative centres, prisons and warehouses to rebuild. Speed was essential so neither of the ambitious new City of London plans submitted by Christopher Wren and John Evelyn was put into effect. Both schemes were too costly and time-consuming. Most buildings were rebuilt on their original sites. But a new awareness had arisen and in 1667 a Rebuilding Act set out strict building regulations. Building materials had to be brick or stone.

St Bride's in Fleet Street was the first City church to be rebuilt. It cost £11,430.

Wren showing his plans for the rebuilding of London's churches.

As Surveyor General, Wren was also responsible for supervising the rebuilding of 51 City churches. This work was not completed until 1686.

The new Globe theatre is the first building in London since the Great Fire to have a thatched roof. The thatch has been specially treated to make sure it will never burn.

A MONUMENT TO THE FIRE

A monument was built to commemorate the fire that consumed the City of London in 1666. It still exists today and attracts visitors from all over the world. The Monument's height is 61.5 metres. This is the same as the distance from the Monument to the site of Thomas Farynor's bakery in Pudding Lane where the fire began.

This carving on the Monument is by Caius Gabriel Cibber, who was also responsible for carvings inside the new St Paul's Cathedral.

At the top of the Monument there is a 'flaming' urn – a lasting symbol of the Great Fire.

Energetic visitors can climb the 311 steps of the spiral staircase inside the Monument. From the top there is a magnificent panorama – St Paul's Cathedral to the west and the Tower of London to the east. Opposite the Monument there is a mural showing the main events of the Great Fire as they happened, while in Pudding Lane a plaque marks the spot where the Great Fire began.

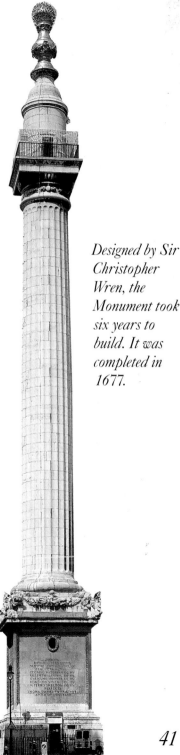

Designed by Sir Christopher Wren, the Monument took six years to build. It was completed in 1677.

NEAR THIS SITE STOOD THE SHOP BELONGING TO THOMAS FARYNER THE KINGS BAKER IN WHICH THE GREAT FIRE OF SEPTEMBER 1666 BEGAN

PRESENTED BY THE WORSHIPFUL COMPANY OF BAKERS TO MARK THE 500th ANNIVERSARY OF THEIR CHARTER GRANTED BY KING HENRY VII IN 1486

41

FIRE INSURANCE

Bfore 1666 insurance against
fire was unknown. But the
Great Fire changed all that – and not just in England
but throughout Europe. One of the immediate
responses to the fire is described in an insurance
encyclopedia: "...the actual adoption of fire insurance
in England, commencing in the metropolis the very
next year; and its general diffusion through Europe...
The lessons of London's greatest fire induced
measures of fire protection in every
principal city and
town in Europe."

*Firemarks were fixed at first-floor level on
house fronts. Firefighters would only deal
with fires at insured properties.*

New fire insurance societies grew up and each had its own fire engines and firefighters. Properties carrying insurance against fire were marked with their society's special metal firemark. By 1690 one in ten houses in London was insured. Property insurance is today's form of the old fire insurance.

This chart shows house insurance rates in the late 17th century.

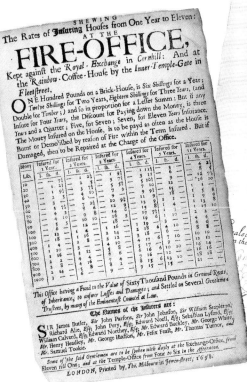

A 17th-century fire insurance certificate.

A Fire Service

N ew and improved fire regulations were issued and London was divided into four areas, each with its own firefighting equipment. By 1832 there were 15 fire insurance companies in London. Firefighting arrangements were still unreliable so the companies decided to pool their resources to form the London Fire Brigade. It had 77 firefighters, 14 fire engines and 13 fire stations.

In the first half of the 18th century, fire engines were often pulled along by hand.

A London firefighter (1696).

By the end of the 18th century, horse-drawn fire engines had been introduced.

Its first superintendent was James Braidwood. In 1861 a large fire broke out to the south of London Bridge. Braidwood died fighting the flames and became a popular hero. The huge insurance claims after this fire almost caused the collapse of the London Fire Brigade. Each part of Britain had its own fire service until the Second World War when a national fire service was set up.

In the fire regulations written into the Rebuilding Act of 1667, householders had to: "...prepare some secure place in their dwelling (not under or near any staircase) to lay in their sea-coal ashes, embers, or any other sort of fire ashes; and that the said ashes be quenched with water every night..."

GLOSSARY

almanac *An annual publication containing statistics about anniversaries, the moon, tides, and so on. Once used to foretell the future.*

astrologer *A person who relates the positions and movements of the planets, sun and moon to human lives.*

charred *Partly burned or scorched.*

combustible *Capable of burning.*

conduit *A pipe or channel for carrying water.*

conflagration *A large, destructive fire or inferno.*

drought *A long period of time with little or no rainfall.*

extinguish *To put out, or quench, flames.*

firebomb *A bomb designed to start a fire, also known as an incendiary.*

firebreak *An area of open land designed to stop the progress of a fire.*

firemark *A metal sign placed on the outside of an insured property after the Great Fire of London to identify the insurer.*

firepost *A meeting point at which firefighters assemble with their firefighting tools.*

inflammable *Liable to catch fire.*

militia *A group of citizens enlisted for military service in times of emergency.*

multi-storeyed *A building with a number of storeys or levels.*

pitch *A dark, sticky substance obtained from tar.*

smoulder *To burn slowly without a flame.*

siphon *A firefighting tool that works by squirting water on to the flames.*

thatch *Roofing made from plant materials such as reeds or straw.*

tinder *Dry wood or other easily combustible materials used to light fires.*

tinderbox *A small container holding tinder, flint and steel, once used to make a flame.*

vigiles *Night-watchmen in Roman times.*

INDEX